leisure & culture DUNDEE

E

Tea Cosies

Lee Ann Garrett

Search Press

First published in 2014

Search Press Limited
Wellwood, North Farm Road,
Tunbridge Wells, Kent TN2 3DR

Text copyright © Lee Ann Garrett 2014

Photographs by Laura Forrester

Photographs and design copyright
© Search Press Ltd 2014

Print ISBN: 978 1 78221 010 8
Epub ISBN: 978 1 78126 202 3
Mobi ISBN: 978 1 78126 203 0

The Publishers and author can accept no
responsibility for any consequences arising from
the information, advice or instructions given in
this publication.

Readers are permitted to reproduce any of
the items in this book for their personal use,
or for the purposes of selling for charity, free of
charge and without the prior permission of the
Publishers. Any use of the items for commercial
purposes is not permitted without the prior
permission of the Publishers.

Suppliers
If you have difficulty in obtaining any of the
materials and equipment mentioned in this book,
then please visit the Search Press website for
details of suppliers: www.searchpress.com

Printed in China

Dedication
*To my husband, Ian, for being my
'number one fan' and encouraging
me to pursue my passion.*

Acknowledgements
Thank you to my loving family and friends,
who cheer me on, support me and who are
there for me in every way. I would also like
to thank Laurie Goldiuk of the Black Lamb
in Port Hope, Canada, for her guidance and
help. A big thank you to Search Press for
producing my book!

Contents

Introduction 4

Knitting know-how 6

Bee Hive 8

Simple Stripes 10

Stars and Moon 12

Watermelon 14

Owl 16

Grapes 18

Nautical 20

Daisy 22

Ladybug 24

Strawberry 26

Cow 28

Butterfly 30

Valentine's Day 32

Pumpkin 34

Christmas 36

Cherry 38

Apple 40

Carrots 42

Bee 44

Falling Leaves 46

Introduction

My love for knitting started when I was eight years old. When my family and I went to visit my grandmother, I'd run to her craft room to see her knitting stash and her current project. On Christmas mornings I couldn't wait to open my favourite gift from her – a box full of knitted doll's clothes! Inspired, I started designing and knitting my own doll's clothes using sequins and bits of fur to embellish them. Over the years I've enjoyed many crafts such as painting, needlepoint, crochet, cross-stitch and sewing. But, I always return to my favourite – knitting.

Which brings me to another of my favourite things: tea. Who doesn't love a cup of hot tea served from a steaming teapot on a cold winter night... or indeed any night! And what better way to keep your teapot warm than one of these colourful tea cosies? This book contains twenty fun, whimsical and easy-to-make designs that will match any décor, mood or special occasion and are perfect for giving as homemade gifts. Many of the tea cosies are inspired by nature: there are vegetable, fruit, butterfly, bee and flower designs as well as the moon and stars. Other designs celebrate the special occasions in our lives, such as Christmas and Valentine's Day.

The book is intended for all, from the beginner to the more experienced knitter, and is ideal for those who want to make quick and easy but accomplished-looking projects. Knitting should be fun, rewarding and relaxing, and I truly hope you enjoy this book. These patterns will allow you to achieve great results in a short period of time, so happy knitting!

Knitting know-how

Use these pages as your essential reference guide – you'll find all the knitting abbreviations used throughout as well as a guide to the embroidery stitches. Remember that all the patterns use the same tension (gauge) and are made to fit a 5–6 cup teapot, see Important Information, below. Conversions for yarn weights and needle sizes are given with every pattern. I have used a US worsted-weight yarn to knit all of the tea cosies in this book. In the UK, this is equivalent to an Aran-weight, also known as 10-ply yarn. Some patterns also include embellishments that have been knitted using double knitting (DK) yarn, which is sometimes referred to as 8-ply. It is recommended that you test the tension using your chosen brand of yarn before you start knitting any of the tea cosies in this book.

Important Information

The tension used in the book – 5 sts = 2.5cm (1in) – gives the cosies a tight, warm fabric. For a looser tension, increase your needle size.

Cosies fit a 5–6 cup teapot.

The bottom of the cosy will roll up naturally and is part of the design.

The first and last stitch in each row is used for the selvage when sewing up the cosy.

I would suggest that you sew the side seams of the tea cosies with mattress stitch for a professional finish. Leave long tails on your pieces of knitting so that you have yarn to use.

Use a grafting stitch, also known as kitchener stitch, to graft the live, top seams on the stitch holders together. Thread a tapestry needle with yarn and weave it through the live stitches to create an almost invisible join.

Abbreviations

beg: beginning

DPN: double-pointed needles

inc: increase (by working into the front and back of the stitch)

k: knit

kfb: knit in front then back of stitch

k2tog: knit two stitches together

knitwise: as though to knit

m1: make one

mm: millimetres

p: purl

p2tog: purl two stitches together

psso: pass slipped stitch over

purlwise: as though to purl

rem: remaining

rep: repeat

sk2po: slip one knitwise, knit two stitches together, pass slipped stitch over

sl: slip, usually slip one stitch

ss: stocking stitch, stockinette stitch

ssk: slip, slip, knit

st(s): stitch(es)

tbl: through back loop

tog: together

yo: yarn over

*: repeat the instructions following the * as many times as specified

Embroidery Stitches

Use this simple stitch guide to help you create the decoration shown throughout the book:

Satin stitch

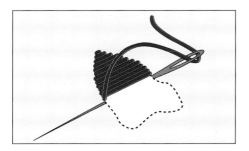

Stem stitch

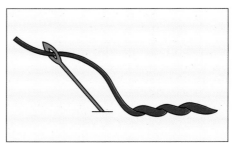

French knots

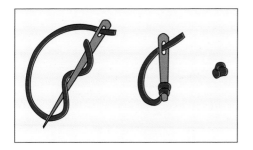

Straight stitch

Overlap four straight stitches per star on the Stars and Moon cosy (page 12).

Use satin stitch to create the irregular black patches on the Cow cosy (page 28).

Bee Hive

Materials:

One ball of honey-coloured worsted-weight (UK Aran) yarn

Tapestry needle

Two stitch holders

Five or six bee buttons

Needles:

One pair 4mm (UK 8, US 6) knitting needles

Tension:

5 sts = 2.5cm (1in)

Instructions:

Make two.

Using honey-coloured yarn and the 4mm (UK 8, US 6) needles, cast on 42 sts.

Work 14 rows in SS ending with a purl row.

Row 15: purl.

Row 16: knit.

Row 17: purl.

Row 18: knit.

Row 19: purl.

Row 20: knit.

Row 21: purl.

Row 22: purl.

Row 23: knit.

Row 24: purl.

Row 25: knit.

Row 26: purl.

Row 27: knit.

Row 28: purl.

Row 29–35: repeat rows 15–21.

Rows 36–42: repeat rows 22–28.

Rows 43–49: repeat rows 15–21.

Row 50: knit.

Row 51: purl.

Shape the top

Row 1: k7, k2tog, *k6, k2tog*, rep from * to * to last st, k1.

Row 2: purl.

Row 3: k6, k2tog, *k5, k2tog*, rep from * to * to last st, k1.

Row 4: purl.

Row 5: k5, k2tog, *k4, k2tog*, rep from * to * to last st, k1.

Row 6: purl.

Row 7: k4, k2tog, *k3, k2tog*, rep from * to * to last st, k1.

Row 8: purl.

Row 9: k3, k2tog, *k2, k2tog*, rep from * to * to last st, k1.

Row 10: purl.

Row 11: k2, k2tog, *k1, k2tog*, rep from * to * to last st, k1.

Row 12: purl.

Row 13: k1, k2tog, *k2tog*, rep from * to * to last st, k1.

Cut yarn and place sts on stitch holder.

Make up the cosy

Place the wrong sides of the cosy together (right sides facing out).

Thread tapestry needle with the tail on the back stitch holder.

Graft the sts on the stitch holders together.

Sew the top

Continue sewing with the tail down one side for 7.5cm (3in).

Fasten off, hide tail in seam.

Repeat on other side of cosy.

Sew the bottom

Thread the tapestry needle with one of the tails of yarn from the cast on edge.

Sew up one side for 4cm (1½in).

Fasten off, hide tail in seam.

Repeat on other side of cosy.

Sew the bee buttons randomly on the cosy.

Getting buzzy

Sew on about five or six bee buttons; arrange them facing in different directions, as though they are buzzing about at random.

Simple Stripes

Materials:

One ball each of cream, red, yellow, navy and turquoise worsted-weight (UK Aran) yarn

Tapestry needle

Two stitch holders

Needles:

One pair 4mm (UK 8, US 6) knitting needles

Tension:

5 sts = 2.5cm (1in)

Instructions:

Make two.

Using cream yarn and 4mm (UK 8, US 6) needles, cast on 42 sts.

Work 12 rows in SS.

Change to navy yarn and work 6 rows.

Change to cream yarn and work 6 rows.

Change to yellow yarn and work 6 rows.

Change to cream yarn and work 6 rows.

Change to red yarn and work 6 rows.

Change to cream yarn and work 6 rows.

Change to turquoise yarn and work 2 rows.

Shape the top

Row 1: continue with turquoise yarn, k7, k2tog, *k6, k2tog*, rep from * to * to last st, k1.

Row 2: purl.

Row 3: k6, k2tog, *k5, k2tog*, rep from * to * to last st, k1.

Row 4: purl.

Row 5: change to cream yarn and k5, k2tog, *k4, k2tog*, rep from * to * to last st, k1.

Row 6: purl.

Row 7: k4, k2tog, *k3, k2tog*, rep from * to * to last st, k1.

Row 8: purl.

Row 9: k3, k2tog, *k2, k2tog*, rep from * to * to last st, k1.

Row 10: purl.

Row 11: k2, k2tog, *k1, k2tog*, rep from * to * to last st, k1.

Row 12: purl.

Row 13: change to navy yarn and k1, k2tog, *k2tog*, rep from * to * to last st, k1.

Row 14: purl.

Row 15: knit.

Row 16: purl.

Row 17: knit.

Cut yarn and place sts on stitch holder.

Make up the cosy

Place the wrong sides of the cosy together (right sides facing out).

Thread tapestry needle with the navy tail on the back stitch holder.

Graft the sts on the stitch holders together.

Sew the top

Continue sewing with the tail down one side for 10cm (4in).

Fasten off and hide tail in the seam.

Repeat on other side of cosy.

Sew the bottom

Thread the tapestry needle with one of the cream tails of yarn from the cast on edge.

Sew up one side for 4cm (1½in).

Fasten off and hide tail in the seam.

Repeat on the other side of cosy.

Stripe swap

Simply adjust the pattern if you want to move or substitute any of the colours given here.

Stars and Moon

Materials:

One ball navy blue worsted-weight
(UK Aran) yarn

Oddments of worsted-weight (UK Aran)
yarn in yellow and white

Tapestry needle

Two stitch holders

Needles:

One pair 4mm (UK 8, US 6) knitting needles

One pair 3.5mm (UK 9, US 4) DPN

Tension:

5 sts = 2.5cm (1in)

Instructions:

Make two.

Using navy blue yarn and 4mm (UK 8, US 6)
needles, cast on 42 sts.

Knit in SS until work measures 16.5cm (6½in)
from the cast on edge.

Shape the top

Row 1: k7, k2tog, *k6, k2tog*, rep from * to * to
last st, k1.

Row 2: purl.

Row 3: k6, k2tog, *k5, k2tog*, rep from * to * to
last st, k1.

Row 4: purl.

Row 5: k5, k2tog, *k4, k2tog*, rep from * to * to
last st, k1.

Row 6: purl.

Row 7: k4, k2tog, *k3, k2tog*, rep from * to * to
last st, k1.

Row 8: purl.

Row 9: k3, k2tog, *k2, k2tog*, rep from * to * to
last st, k1.

Row 10: purl.

Row 11: k2, k2tog, *k1, k2tog*, rep from * to *
to last st, k1.

Row 12: purl.

Row 13: knit.

Row 14: purl.

Row 15: k1, k2tog, *k2tog*, rep from * to * to
last st, k1.

Row 16: purl.

Row 17: knit.

Row 18: purl.

Row 19: k1, k2tog, k1, k2tog, k1.

Row 20: purl.

Row 21: knit.

Row 22: purl.

Row 23: knit.

Cut yarn and place sts on stitch holder.

Make up the cosy

Place the wrong sides of the cosy together
(right sides facing out).

Thread tapestry needle with the navy blue tail
on the back stitch holder.

Graft the sts on the stitch holders together.

Sew the top

Continue sewing with the tail down one side
for 10cm (4in).

Fasten off and hide tail in the seam.

Repeat on other side of cosy.

Sew the bottom

Thread the tapestry needle with one of the
navy blue tails of yarn from the cast on edge.

Sew up one side for 4cm (1½in).

Fasten off and hide tail in the seam.

Repeat on the other side of cosy.

Make the moon

Using white yarn and 3.5mm (UK 9, US 4) DPN,
cast on 2 sts.

Rows 1–7: knit.

Row 8: cast on 1 st using backward loop cast on.

Rows 9–16: knit.

Row 17: cast on 1 st using backward loop
cast on.

Row 18–25: knit.

Row 26: k2tog across row.

Row 27–33: knit.

Row 34: k2tog.

Fasten off.

Work in ends neatly.

Make the string

Using navy blue yarn and 3.5mm (UK 9, US 4) DPN, cast on 2 sts.

Row 1: k2; do not turn but slide sts to other end of needle.

Repeat this row until work measures 2.5cm (1in).

Fasten off.

Sew one end of tail to the top of the moon and the other to the top of the cosy.

Work in ends neatly.

Make the stars

Using yellow yarn and small, straight stitches, embroider stars on the front of the cosy.

Super stars

When sewing your stars, create as many as you like but try to keep them equally spaced and similar in size.

Watermelon

Materials:

One ball each of red, green and white worsted-weight (UK Aran) yarn

Oddment of black yarn

Tapestry needle

Two stitch holders

Needles:

One pair 4mm (UK 8, US 6) knitting needles

Tension:

5 sts = 2.5cm (1in)

Instructions:

Make two.

Using green yarn and 4mm (UK 8, US 6) needles, cast on 42 sts.

Work 14 rows in SS.

Change to white yarn and work 8 rows.

Change to red yarn and work until cosy measures 16.5cm (6½in) from the cast on edge.

Shape the top

Row 1: k7, k2tog, *k6, k2tog*, rep from * to * last st, k1.

Row 2: purl.

Row 3: k6, k2tog, *k5, k2tog*, rep from * to * last st, k1.

Row 4: purl.

Row 5: k5, k2tog, *k4, k2tog*, rep from * to * last st, k1.

Row 6: purl.

Row 7: k4, k2tog, *k3, k2tog*, rep from * to * last st, k1.

Row 8: purl.

Row 9: k3, k2tog, *k2, k2tog*, rep from * to * last st, k1.

Row 10: purl.

Row 11: k2, k2tog, *k1, k2tog*, rep from * to * to last st, k1.

Row 12: purl.

Row 13: k1, k2tog, *k2tog*, rep from * to * to last st, k1.

Cut yarn and place sts on stitch holder.

Make up the cosy

Place the wrong sides of the cosy together (right sides facing out).

Thread tapestry needle with the red tail on the back stitch holder.

Graft the sts on the stitch holders together.

Sew the top

Continue sewing with the tail down one side for 7.5cm (3in).

Fasten off and hide tail in the seam.

Repeat on other side of cosy.

Sew the bottom

Thread the tapestry needle with one of the green tails of yarn from the cast on edge.

Sew up one side for 4cm (1½in).

Fasten off and hide tail in the seam.

Repeat on the other side of cosy.

Make the seeds

Using black yarn, embroider small, 'V'-shaped patterns randomly around the cosy.

Juicy fruit

Use small, straight, diagonal stitches to create your watermelon seeds – to achieve the effect shown here, make the 'V' shapes two stitches wide and one or two stitches tall.

Owl

Materials:

One ball brown or colour of choice worsted-weight (UK Aran) yarn

Oddments of worsted-weight (UK Aran) yarn in cream, yellow and black

Two black buttons

Tapestry needle

Needles:

One pair 4mm (UK 8, US 6) knitting needles

One pair 4.5mm (UK 7, US 7) DPN

Tension:

5 sts = 2.5cm (1in)

Instructions:

Using brown yarn and 4mm (UK 8, US 6) needles, cast on 42 sts.

Knit in SS until work measures 42cm (16½in) from the cast on edge.

Make up the cosy

Fold the wrong sides of the cosy together (right sides facing out).

Sew the top

Thread a tapestry needle with one of the brown tails at the top of the cosy.

Sew down one side for approximately 6.5cm (2½in).

Fasten off, hide tail in seam.

Repeat on other side of cosy.

Sew the bottom

Thread the tapestry needle with one of the brown tails of yarn from the cast on edge.

Sew up one side for approximately 4cm (1½in).

Fasten off, hide tail in seam.

Repeat on the other side of cosy.

Make the eye

Using cream yarn and the 4.5mm (UK 7, US 7) DPN, cast on 6 sts.

Row 1: knit.

Row 2: kfb in each st.

Rows 3–16: knit.

Row 17: k2tog across row.

Cast off those 6 sts.

Make the centre of the eye

Using yellow yarn and the 4.5mm (UK 7, US 7) DPN, cast on 3 sts.

Row 1: kfb in each st.

Row 2: kfb in each st.

Row 3: *k1, kfb*, repeat from * to * to end of row.

Row 4: knit.

Cast off.

Shape into a circle and sew seam.

Make the pupils

Sew a black button to the middle of the centre eye.

Make the beak

Using black yarn and the 4.5mm (UK 7, US 7) DPN, cast on 2 sts.

Row 1: knit.

Row 2: purl.

Row 3: kfb, kfb.

Row 4: purl.

Row 5: knit.

Row 6: purl.

Row 7: kfb, k2, kfb.

Row 8: purl.

Row 9: knit.

Row 10: purl.

Row 11: kfb, k4, kfb.

Row 12: purl.

Row 13: knit.

Row 14: purl.

Row 15: k2tog across row.

Cast off purlwise.

Make the ear tufts

Make two.

Take a piece of cardboard about 8cm (3in) wide and wrap black yarn around it about ten times.

Slide the yarn loop off the cardboard and, with another piece of black yarn, tie a knot around the loop about 2cm (¾in) from one end. Wind the yarn tightly up to the top then down around this 2cm (¾in). Secure the thread, then sew the tufts on to the points of the tea cosy and trim the ends.

Feathered friend

Using a white-flecked brown yarn gives a lovely rustic look to the cosy, but don't be afraid to experiment with bright or bold shades to create a more colourful character!

Grapes

Materials:

One ball purple worsted-weight (UK Aran) yarn

Oddment of worsted-weight (UK Aran) yarn in green

Tapestry needle

Two stitch holders

Needles:

One pair 4mm (UK 8, US 6) knitting needles

One pair 4.5mm (UK 7, US 7) DPN

Tension:

5 sts = 2.5cm (1in)

Instructions:

Make two.

Using purple yarn and 4mm (UK 8, US 6) needles, cast on 42 sts.

Knit in SS until work measures 15cm (6in) from the cast on edge.

Shape the top

Row 1: k7, k2tog, *k6, k2tog*, rep from * to * to last st, k1.

Row 2: purl.

Row 3: k6, k2tog, *k5, k2tog*, rep from * to * to last st, k1.

Row 4: purl.

Row 5: k5, k2tog, *k4, k2tog*, rep from * to * to last st, k1.

Row 6: purl.

Row 7: k4, k2tog, *k3, k2tog*, rep from * to * to last st, k1.

Row 8: purl.

Row 9: k3, k2tog, *k2, k2tog*, rep from * to * to last st, k1.

Row 10: purl.

Row 11: k2, k2tog, *k1, k2tog*, rep from * to * to last st, k1.

Row 12: purl.

Row 13: k1, k2tog, *k2tog*, rep from * to * to last st, k1.

Row 14: purl.

Row 15: change to green for stem and k1, k2tog, k1, k2tog, k1.

Row 16: purl.

Row 17: knit.

Row 18: purl.

Row 19: knit.

Cut yarn and place sts on stitch holder.

Make up the cosy

Place the wrong sides of the cosy together (right sides facing out).

Thread tapestry needle with the green tail on the back stitch holder.

Graft the sts on the stitch holders together.

Sew the stem

Continuing with the green tail of yarn, sew down one side of the stem. Fasten off and hide tail in seam.

Repeat on other side of stem.

Sew the top

Thread a tapestry needle with one of the purple tails at the top of the cosy.

Sew down one side for 7.5cm (3in).

Fasten off and hide tail in the seam.

Repeat on other side of cosy.

Sew the bottom

Thread the tapestry needle with one of the purple tails of yarn from the cast on edge.

Sew up one side for 4cm (1½in).

Fasten off and hide tail in the seam.

Repeat on the other side of cosy.

Make the grapes

Make about 34.

Using purple yarn and 4.5mm (UK 7, US 7) DPN, cast on 3 sts.

Row 1: kfb in each st.

Row 2: knit.

Row 3: k2tog across row.

Row 4: sk2po.

Cut yarn and pull through remaining sts.

Using the tapestry needle and tails, sew grapes randomly on to cosy.

Make the vines

Make six.

Using green worsted-weight yarn and 4.5mm (UK 7, US 7) DPN, cast on 24 sts.

Cast off the 24 sts.

Fasten off.

Twist vines to help make them curl.

Attach the vines

Position the vines to the base of the stem and sew in place.

Work in ends neatly.

Grape expectations

The bobbly texture and wiggly vines make this a wonderfully tactile, playful cosy.

Nautical

Materials:

One ball each of navy and white worsted-weight (UK Aran) yarn

Oddment of red worsted-weight (UK Aran) yarn

Two stitch holders

Needles:

One pair 4mm (UK 8, US 6) knitting needles

One pair 4.5mm (UK 7, US 7) DPN

Tension:

5 sts = 2.5cm (1in)

Instructions:

Make two.

Using navy yarn and 4mm (UK 8, US 6) needles, cast on 42 sts.

Work 16 rows in SS.

Change to white yarn and work 8 rows.

Change to navy yarn and work 8 rows.

Change to white yarn and work 8 rows.

Change to navy yarn and work 8 rows.

Change to white yarn and work 2 rows.

Shape the top

Row 1: continue with white yarn, k7, k2tog, *k6, k2tog*, rep from * to * to last st, k1.

Row 2: purl.

Row 3: k6, k2tog, *k5, k2tog*, rep from * to * to last st, k1.

Row 4: purl.

Row 5: k5, k2tog, *k4, k2tog*, rep from * to * to last st, k1.

Row 6: purl.

Row 7: k4, k2tog, *k3, k2tog*, rep from * to * to last st, k1.

Row 8: purl.

Row 9: k3, k2tog, *k2, k2tog*, rep from * to * to last st, k1.

Row 10: purl.

Row 11: change to navy yarn and k2, k2tog, *k1, k2tog*, rep from * to * to last st, k1.

Row 12: purl.

Row 13: k1, k2tog, *k2tog*, rep from * to * to last st, k1.

Row 14: purl.

Row 15: change to red yarn and k1, k2tog, k1, k2tog, k1.

Row 16: purl.

Row 17: knit.

Repeat rows 16 and 17 until 'knot' measures 15cm (6in).

Cut yarn and place sts on stitch holder.

Make up the cosy

Place the wrong sides of the cosy together (right sides facing out).

Thread tapestry needle with the red tail on the back stitch holder.

Graft the sts on the stitch holders together.

Sew the top red section

Continuing with the red tail of yarn, sew down one side of the red section.

Fasten off and hide tail in seam.

Repeat on other side of the red section.

Sew the top

Thread a tapestry needle with one of the navy tails at the top of the cosy.

Sew down one side for 7.5cm (3in).

Fasten off and hide tail in the seam.

Repeat on other side of cosy.

Sew the bottom

Thread the tapestry needle with one of the navy tails of yarn from the cast on edge.

Sew 4cm (1½in) up one side.

Fasten off and hide tail in the seam.

Repeat on the other side of cosy.

Tie red tail in a knot on the top of the cosy.

Make the life ring

Using white yarn and the 4.5mm (UK 7, US 7) DPN, cast on 4 sts.

Row 1: *k4; do not turn but slide sts to other

end of needle*, rep from * to * seven times.

Change to red yarn.

Row 2: *k4; do not turn but slide sts to other end of needle*, rep from * to * three times.

Change to white.

Repeat rows 1–2 three times.

(Note: carry red and white yarn up the back of the life ring as you knit).

Fasten off and sew together to form ring.

Work in ends neatly.

Make the string

Using red yarn and 4.5mm (UK 7, US 7) DPN, cast on 2 sts.

Row 1: k2; do not turn but slide sts to other end of needle.

Repeat this row until work measures approximately 6.5cm (2½in).

Fasten off.

Using one of the tails, sew string to the top of the life ring. With the other tail, sew string below the knot.

Work in ends neatly.

Tea by the sea

This gorgeous cosy would add a cute finishing touch to a vintage tea party.

Daisy

Materials:

One ball of yellow worsted-weight (UK Aran) yarn

Oddment of green worsted-weight (UK Aran) yarn

Oddment of white yarn

Tapestry needle

Two stitch holders

Needles:

One pair 4mm (UK 8, US 6) knitting needles

One pair 4mm (UK 8, US 6) DPN

One pair 3.5mm (UK 9, US 4) knitting needles

One pair 3.25mm (UK 10, US 3) knitting needles

Tension:

5 sts = 2.5cm (1in)

Instructions:

Make two.

Using yellow yarn and 4mm (UK 8, US 6) needles cast on 42 sts.

Knit in SS until work measures 16.5cm (6½in) from the cast on edge.

Shape the top

Row 1: k7, k2tog, *k6, k2tog*, rep from * to * to last st, k1.

Row 2: purl.

Row 3: k6, k2tog, *k5, k2tog*, rep from * to * to last st, k1.

Row 4: purl.

Row 5: k5, k2tog, *k4, k2tog*, rep from * to * to last st, k1.

Row 6: purl.

Row 7: k4, k2tog, *k3, k2tog*, rep from * to * to last st, k1.

Row 8: purl.

Row 9: k3, k2tog, *k2, k2tog*, rep from * to * to last st, k1.

Row 10: purl.

Row 11: k2, k2tog, *k1, k2tog*, rep from * to * to last st, k1.

Row 12: purl.

Row 13: k1, k2tog, *k2tog*, rep from * to * to last st, k1.

Row 14: change to green for stem and k1, k2tog, k1, k2tog, k1.

Row 15: purl.

Row 16: knit.

Row 17: purl.

Row 18: knit.

Row 19: purl.

Row 20: knit.

Do not cut yarn.

Place sts on stitch holder.

Make up the cosy

Place the wrong sides of the cosy together (right sides facing out).

Sew the stem

Thread a tapestry needle with one of the green tails of the stem.

Sew down one side.

Fasten off, hide tail in seam. Repeat on other side of stem.

Sew the top

Using one of the tails of the yellow yarn, sew down one side of the cosy for 7.5cm (3in).

Fasten off, hide tail in seam.

Repeat on other side of cosy.

Sew the bottom

Thread the tapestry needle with one of the yellow tails of yarn from the cast on edge.

Sew up one side for 4cm (1½in).

Fasten off, hide tail in seam.

Repeat on other side of cosy.

Make the stalks

Slip first st from stitch holder onto one of the 4mm (UK 8, US 6) DPN.

Row 1: continuing with the green yarn, work this stitch only and cast on 24 sts using the backward loop cast on.

Row 2: cast off the same 24 sts as tight as possible to make 'stalk' curl.

Row 3: knit next st from stitch holder.

Row 4: cast off first st over the second st (1 st remains on needle).

Repeat rows 1–4 across this st and the remaining 3 sts on the stitch holder.

Cut yarn leaving a 25cm (10in) tail.

Fasten off.

Repeat the above on the sts on the other st holder.

Sew the stalks together

Using the picture as a guideline, thread green tail through tapestry needle and wind yarn tightly around the ten stalks of the cosy to hold them securely together.

Hide tail down through middle of the stalks and fasten under cosy – this helps the stalks to stand up straight.

Work in ends neatly.

Make the daisy

Leave extra long tails for sewing flower.

Using the green yarn and 3.5mm (UK 9, US 4) knitting needles, cast on 10 sts.

Change to white yarn and knit across these sts.

Place sts on stitch holder.

Row 1: knit the first st on the holder onto the 3.5mm (UK 9, US 4) needle. Slide st to the right hand side of the needle and cast on 14 sts.

Row 2: cast off these 14 sts. 1 st remains on the needle.

Row 3: knit the next st off of the st holder (2 sts on needle) and cast off this st.

Row 4: slide this st to the right hand side of the needle and cast on 14 sts.

Repeat rows 3 and 4 until all the sts on the st holder are worked.

Cut yarn and fasten off.

Form the daisy into a circle and sew the centre of the flower together.

Using one of the white tails, sew the top of each petal to the centre of the flower.

Hide ends.

Make the string

Using green yarn and 3.25mm (UK 10, US 3) knitting needles, cast on 2 sts.

Row 1: k2; do not turn but slide sts to other end of needle.

Repeat this row until work measures approximately 17.5cm (7in).

Fasten off.

Using one of the tails, sew string to the top of the daisy.

With the other tail, sew string below the stem of the cosy.

Work in ends neatly.

Flower power

*Ideal for a summer tea party:
adapt the colours to create
your favourite flowers.*

Ladybug

Materials:

One ball each of black and red worsted-
weight (UK Aran) yarn

Tapestry needle

Two stitch holders

Needles:

One pair 4mm (UK 8, US 6) knitting needles

One pair 4.5mm (UK 7, US 7) DPN

Tension:

5 sts = 2.5cm (1in)

Instructions:

Make two.

Using black yarn and 4mm (UK 8, US 6) needles,
cast on 42 sts.

Work 14 rows in SS.

Change to red yarn and knit until work
measures 16.5cm (6½in) from the cast on edge.

Shape the top

Row 1: change to black yarn and k7, k2tog, *k6,
k2tog*, rep from * to * to last st, k1.

Row 2: purl.

Row 3: k6, k2tog, *k5, k2tog*, rep from * to * to
last st, k1.

Row 4: purl.

Row 5: k5, k2tog, *k4, k2tog*, rep from * to * to
last st, k1.

Row 6: purl.

Row 7: k4, k2tog, *k3, k2tog*, rep from * to * to
last st, k1.

Row 8: purl.

Row 9: k3, k2tog, *k2, k2tog*, rep from * to * to
last st, k1.

Row 10: purl.

Row 11: k2, k2tog, *k1, k2tog*, rep from * to *
to last st, k1.

Row 12: purl.

Row 13: k1, k2tog, *k2tog*, rep from * to * to
last st, k1.

Cut yarn and place sts on stitch holder.

Make up the cosy

Place the wrong sides of the cosy together
(right sides facing out).

Thread tapestry needle with the black tail on
the back stitch holder.

Graft the sts on the stitch holders together.

Sew the top

Continue sewing down one side for 7.5cm (3in).

Fasten off and hide tail in the seam.

Repeat on other side of cosy.

Sew the bottom

Thread the tapestry needle with one of the
black tails of yarn from the cast on edge.

Sew up one side for 4cm (1½in).

Fasten off and hide tail in the seam.

Repeat on the other side of cosy.

Make the wing division

Using black yarn and stem stitch, embroider
the wing division up the centre of the cosy.

Make the spots

Make six.

Using black yarn and 4.5mm (UK 7, US 7) DPN,
cast on 3 sts.

Row 1: kfb in each st.

Row 2: knit.

Row 3: k2tog across row.

Row 4: sk2po.

Cut yarn and pull through remaining sts.

Using the tapestry needle and tails, sew spots
on cosy.

Make the antennae

Make two.

Measure 2.5cm (1in) from centre top of cosy.

Using black yarn and 4.5mm (UK 7, US 7) DPN,
pick up and knit 4 sts.

Row 1: k4; do not turn but slide sts to other end
of needle.

Repeat this row until work measures 6cm (2½in).

Next row: kfb, k2, kfb, (6 sts); do not turn but

slide sts to other end of needle.

Work two more rows even with these 6 sts.

Cut yarn leaving a 15cm (6in) tail.

With tapestry needle pull tail across the back and through the 6 sts.

Pull the tail down through the centre of the cord – pull it tight enough that the antenna stands upright.

Secure tail underneath the cosy.

Repeat for other antenna.

Dot to dot
Attach the spots in whatever arrangement you want – you could even create more than six if you like.

Strawberry

Materials:

One ball red worsted-weight (UK Aran) yarn

Oddments of worsted-weight (UK Aran) yarn in green and white

Tapestry needle

Two stitch holders

Needles:

One pair 4mm (UK 8, US 6) knitting needles

One pair 4mm (UK 8, US 6) DPN

Tension:

5 sts = 2.5cm (1in)

Instructions:

Make two.

Using red yarn and 4mm (UK 8, US 6) needles, cast on 42 sts.

Knit in SS until work measures 15cm (6in) from the cast on edge.

Shape the top

Row 1: k7, k2tog, *k6, k2tog*, rep from * to * to last st, k1.

Row 2: purl.

Row 3: k6, k2tog, *k5, k2tog*, rep from * to * to last st, k1.

Row 4: purl.

Row 5: k5, k2tog, *k4, k2tog*, rep from * to * to last st, k1.

Row 6: purl.

Row 7: k4, k2tog, *k3, k2tog*, rep from * to * to last st, k1.

Row 8: purl.

Row 9: k3, k2tog, *k2, k2tog*, rep from * to * to last st, k1.

Row 10: purl.

Row 11: k2, k2tog, *k1, k2tog*, rep from * to * to last st, k1.

Row 12: purl.

Row 13: k1, k2tog, *k2tog*, rep from * to * to last st, k1.

Row 14: purl.

Row 15: change to green for stem and k1, k2tog, k1, k2tog, k1.

Row 16: purl.

Row 17: knit.

Row 18: purl.

Row 19: knit.

Cut yarn and place sts on stitch holder.

Make up the cosy

Place the wrong sides of the cosy together (right sides facing out).

Thread tapestry needle with the green tail on the back stitch holder.

Graft the sts on the stitch holders together.

Sew the stem

Continuing with the green tail of yarn, sew down one side of the stem. Fasten off and hide tail in seam.

Repeat on other side of stem.

Sew the top

Thread a tapestry needle with one of the red tails at the top of the cosy.

Sew down one side for 7.5cm (3in).

Fasten off and hide tail in the seam.

Repeat on other side of cosy.

Sew the bottom

Thread the tapestry needle with one of the red tails of yarn from the cast on edge.

Sew up one side for 4cm (1½in).

Fasten off and hide tail in the seam.

Repeat on the other side of cosy.

Make the leaves

Make five.

Using green yarn and the 4mm (UK 8, US 6) DPN, cast on 2 sts.

Rows 1–8: knit.

Row 9: k1, m1, k1.

Rows 10–15: knit.

Row 16: k1, m1, k1, m1, k1.

Row 17–22: knit.

Row 23: k1, m1, k3, m1, k1.

Rows 24–27: knit.

Row 28: k1, k2tog, k1, k2tog, k1.

Row 29: k2tog, k1, k2tog.

Row 30: sk2po.

Fasten off.

Attach the leaves

Position the leaves on the base of the stem and sew in place.

Work in ends neatly.

Make the seeds

Using white yarn, embroider small, 'V'-shaped patterns randomly around the cosy.

Get fruity

Why not enjoy this tempting tea cosy with fruity cakes and tea?

Cow

Materials:

One ball white worsted-weight (UK Aran) yarn

Oddment of worsted-weight (UK Aran) yarn in black

Tapestry needle

Two stitch holders

Instructions:

Make two.

Using white yarn and 4mm (UK 8, US 6) needles, cast on 42 sts.

Knit in SS until work measures 16.5cm (6½in) from the cast on edge.

Shape the top

Row 1: k7, k2tog, *k6, k2tog* rep from * to * to last st, k1.

Row 2: purl.

Row 3: k6, k2tog, *k5, k2tog*, rep from * to * to last st, k1.

Row 4: purl.

Row 5: k5, k2tog, *k4, k2tog*, rep from * to * to last st, k1.

Row 6: purl.

Row 7: k4, k2tog, *k3, k2tog*, rep from * to * to last st, k1.

Row 8: purl.

Row 9: k3, k2tog, *k2, k2tog*, rep from * to * to last st, k1.

Row 10: purl.

Row 11: k2, k2tog, *k1, k2tog*, rep from * to * to last st, k1.

Row 12: purl.

Row 13: k1, k2tog, *k2tog*, rep from * to * to last st, k1.

Row 14: purl.

Row 15: change to black yarn for tail and k1, k2tog, k1, k2tog, k1.

Rows 16–46: continue in SS.

Cut yarn and place sts on stitch holder.

Make up the cosy

Place the wrong sides of the cosy together (right sides facing out).

Needles:

One pair 4mm (UK 8, US 6) knitting needles

Tension:

5 sts = 2.5cm (1in)

Sew the top

Thread a tapestry needle with one of the white tails at the top of the cosy.

Sew down one side for 7.5cm (3in).

Fasten off and hide tail in the seam.

Repeat on other side of cosy.

Sew the bottom

Thread the tapestry needle with one of the tails of yarn from the cast on edge.

Sew 4cm (1½in) up one side.

Fasten off, hide tail in seam.

Repeat on other side of cosy.

Make the tail

Cut ten strands of white yarn about 20cm (8in) long.

Remove first st off one of the st holders.

Using tapestry needle, thread one strand of the white yarn.

Pull yarn carefully through the st doubling yarn over.

Continue pulling white strands of yarn through each st on the stitch holder.

Repeat above directions on the other stitch holder.

Thread tapestry needle with one of the black tails of yarn at the top of the cow tail and sew down one side of the cow tail.

Repeat on the other side.

Hide yarn ends.

Tie the white strands of yarn in a knot at the end of the black tail.

Trim ends to desired length.

Make the spots

Using black yarn and the tapestry needle embroider satin stitch 'patches' randomly on the cosy in different sizes.

Farmyard fun
*This quirky cow-print cosy
is ideal for animal lovers!*

Butterfly

Materials:

One ball sky-blue worsted-weight (UK Aran) yarn

Oddments of double knitting (DK) weight yarn in pink, yellow and black

Oddment of white 'fuzzy' novelty yarn

Tapestry needle

Two stitch holders

Needles:

One pair 4mm (UK 8, US 6) knitting needles

One pair 3.5mm (UK 9, US 4) DPN

Tension:

5 sts = 2.5cm (1in)

Instructions:

Make two.

Using sky-blue yarn and 4mm (UK 8, US 6) needles, cast on 42 sts.

Knit in SS until work measures 16.5cm (6½in) from the cast on edge.

Shape the top

Row 1: k7, k2tog, *k6, k2tog*, rep from * to * to last st, k1.

Row 2: purl.

Row 3: k6, k2tog, *k5, k2tog*, rep from * to * to last st, k1.

Row 4: purl.

Row 5: k5, k2tog, *k4, k2tog*, rep from * to * to last st, k1.

Row 6: purl.

Row 7: k4, k2tog, *k3, k2tog*, rep from * to * to last st, k1.

Row 8: purl.

Row 9: k3, k2tog, *k2, k2tog*, rep from * to * to last st, k1.

Row 10: purl.

Row 11: k2, k2tog, *k1, k2tog*, rep from * to * to last st, k1.

Row 12: purl.

Row 13: knit.

Row 14: purl.

Row 15: k1, k2tog, *k2tog*, rep from * to * to last st, k1.

Row 16: purl.

Row 17: knit.

Row 18: purl.

Row 19: k1, k2tog, k1, k2tog, k1.

Row 20: purl.

Row 21: knit.

Row 22: purl.

Row 23: knit.

Cut yarn and place sts on stitch holder.

Make up the cosy

Place the wrong sides of the cosy together (right sides facing out).

Thread tapestry needle with the sky-blue tail on the back stitch holder.

Graft the sts on the stitch holders together.

Sew the top

Continue sewing with the tail down one side for 10cm (4in).

Fasten off, hide tail in seam.

Repeat on other side of cosy.

Sew the bottom

Thread the tapestry needle with one of the blue tails of yarn from the cast on edge.

Sew up one side for 4cm (1½in).

Fasten off, hide tail in seam.

Repeat on other side of cosy.

Make the wings

Make two.

Using pink yarn and 3.5mm (UK 9, US 4) DPN, cast on 9 sts.

Row 1: knit.

Row 2: knit.

Row 3: k1, kfb, k5, kfb, k1.

Row 4: knit.

Row 5: k1, kfb, k7, kfb, k1.

Row 6: knit.

Row 7: k1, kfb, k9, kfb, k1.

Row 8: k7, k2tog, k6.

Do not cut yarn.

Make the bottom wing

Work on first 7 sts only.

Row 1: k1, k2tog, k1, k2tog, k1.

Row 2: k2, k2tog, k1.

Row 3: k1, k2tog, k1.

Row 4: knit.

Fasten off.

Make the top wing

Join yarn and continue with the remaining sts.

Row 1: k1, k2tog, k1, k2tog, k1.

Row 2: k1, k2tog, k2.

Row 3: k1, k2tog, k1.

Row 4: knit.

Fasten off.

Repeat above instructions for the other wing.

Using yellow yarn and tapestry needle, embroider one French knot in each corner of the wing.

Make the body

Using yellow yarn and 3.5mm (UK 9, US 4) DPN cast on 3 sts.

Row 1: k3; do not turn but slide sts to other end of needle.

Repeat this row until work measures 5cm (2in).

Make up the butterfly

Sew the two wings together; sew the yellow body down the middle of the two wings.

Sew on two strands of black yarn to make antennae.

Work ends in neatly.

Make the string

Using sky-blue yarn and 3.5mm (UK 9, US 4) DPN, cast on 2 sts.

Row 1: k2; do not turn but slide sts to other end of needle.

Repeat this row until work measures 7.5cm (3in).

Fasten off.

Sew one end of tail to the top of the butterfly and the other to the top of the cosy.

Work in ends neatly.

Make the clouds

Using the white novelty yarn and tapestry needle, embroider groups of satin stitches randomly on cosy for the clouds.

Summertime style

This whimsical cosy would suit a picnic on a warm summer's day.

Valentine's Day

Materials:

One ball each white and red worsted-weight (UK Aran) yarn

Tapestry needle

Two stitch holders

Polyester wadding

Needles:

One pair 4mm (UK 8, US 6) knitting needles

One pair of 4mm (UK 8, US 6) DPN

One pair 3.25mm (UK 10, US 3) DPN

Tension:

5 sts = 2.5cm (1in)

Instructions:

Make two.

Using red yarn and 4mm (UK 8, US 6) needles, cast on 42 sts.

Work 14 rows in SS.

Change to white yarn and continue in SS until cosy measures 15cm (6in) from the cast on edge.

Shape the top

Row 1: k7, k2tog, *k6, k2tog*, rep from * to * to last st, k1.

Row 2: purl.

Row 3: k6, k2tog, *k5, k2tog*, rep from * to * to last st, k1.

Row 4: purl.

Row 5: knit.

Row 6: purl.

Row 7: k4, yo, k2tog, k4, yo, k2tog, k4, yo, k2tog.

Row 8: purl.

Row 9: knit.

Row 10: purl.

Change to red and continue with SS for 14 rows.

Cast off.

Make up the cosy

Place the wrong sides of the cosy together (right sides facing out).

Sew the top

Thread tapestry needle with one of the white tails.

Sew 6cm (2½in) down one side, starting at the first white row.

Fasten off, hide tail in seam.

Repeat on other side of cosy.

Sew the bottom

Thread the tapestry needle with one of the red tails of yarn from the cast on edge.

Sew up one side for 4cm (1½in).

Fasten off, hide tail in seam.

Repeat on other side of cosy.

Make the hearts

For two hearts make four heart shapes.

Using red yarn and 3.25mm (UK 10, US 3) needles, cast on 3 sts.

Row 1: purl.

Row 2: k1, yo, k1, yo, k1.

Row 3: purl.

Row 4: k1, yo, k3, yo, k1.

Row 5: purl.

Row 6: k1, yo, k5, yo, k1.

Row 7: purl.

Row 8: k1, yo, k7, yo, k1.

Row 9: purl.

Row 10: k1, yo, k9, yo, k1.

Row 11: p5, p2tog, p6.

Work the top of the hearts following the directions below.

Do not cut yarn.

Make the first lobe

Row 1: k1, ssk, k1, k2tog.

Slip remaining 6 sts onto st holder.

Row 2: p1, p2tog, p1.

Row 3: knit.

Row 4: sl1 purlwise, p2tog, psso.

Cut yarn and pull through st.

Make the second lobe

Slip 6 sts from st holder onto needle.

Join yarn.

Row 1: k1, ssk, k1, k2tog.

Row 2: p1, p2tog, p1.

Row 3: knit.

Row 4: sl 1 purlwise, p2tog, psso.

Cut yarn and pull through st.

With tails and tapestry needle, sew two hearts together (right sides facing out) leaving a small opening at the top of the heart.

Lightly stuff hearts with wadding. Finish sewing.

Make the hanging cord

Using red yarn and the 4mm (UK 8, US 6) DPN, cast on 3 sts.

Row 1: k3; do not turn but slide sts to other end of needle.

Repeat this row until work measures approximately 25cm (10in).

Fasten off.

Weave cord through eyelets at the top of the cosy. Make sure both ends come out of the same eyelet opening.

Sew cord ends to hearts, pull cord tight and tie cord into a knot.

Love is in the air
What could be better than a steaming mug of tea to warm your heart and hands on Valentine's day?

Pumpkin

Materials:

One ball orange worsted-weight (UK Aran) yarn

Oddments of worsted-weight (UK Aran) yarn in brown and green

Tapestry needle

Two stitch holders

Needles:

One pair 4mm (UK 8, US 6) knitting needles

One pair 4mm (UK 8, US 6) DPN

Tension:

5 sts = 2.5cm (1in)

Instructions:

Make two.

Using orange yarn and 4mm (UK 8, US 6) needles, cast on 42 sts.

Knit in SS for 12 rows.

Row 13: k4, p1, *k7, p1* repeat from * to *, until last 5 sts then p1, k4.

Row 14: purl.

Repeat rows 13 and 14 until work measures 15cm (6in) from the cast on edge.

Shape the top

Row 1: k7, k2tog, *k6, k2tog* rep from * to * to last st, k1.

Row 2: purl.

Row 3: k6, k2tog, *k5, k2tog*, rep from * to * to last st, k1.

Row 4: purl.

Row 5: k5, k2tog, *k4, k2tog*, rep from * to * to last st, k1.

Row 6: purl.

Row 7: k4, k2tog, *k3, k2tog*, rep from * to * to last st, k1.

Row 8: purl.

Row 9: k3, k2tog, *k2, k2tog*, rep from * to * to last st, k1.

Row 10: purl.

Row 11: k2, k2tog, *k1, k2tog*, rep from * to * to last st, k1.

Row 12: purl.

Row 13: k1, k2tog, *k2tog*, rep from * to * to last st, k1.

Row 14: purl.

Row 15: change to brown yarn and k1, k2tog, k1, k2tog, k1.

Row 16: purl.

Row 17: knit.

Row 18: purl.

Row 19: knit.

Cut yarn and place sts on stitch holder.

Make up the cosy

Place the wrong sides of the cosy together (right sides out).

Thread tapestry needle with the brown tail on the back stitch holder.

Graft the sts on the stitch holders together.

Sew the stem

Continuing with the brown tail of yarn, sew down one side of the stem. Fasten off and hide tail in seam.

Repeat on other side of stem.

Sew the top

Thread a tapestry needle with one of the orange tails at the top of the cosy.

Sew down one side for 7.5cm (3in).

Fasten off, hide tail in seam.

Repeat on other side of cosy.

Sew the bottom

Thread the tapestry needle with one of the orange tails of yarn from the cast on edge.

Sew up one side for 4cm (1½in).

Fasten off, hide tail in seam.

Repeat on other side of cosy.

Make the leaf

Using green yarn and the 4mm (UK 8, US 6) DPN, cast on 4 sts.

Row 1: purl.

Row 2: k2, kfb, k1.

Row 3: purl.

Row 4: k2, kfb, k2.

Row 5: purl.

Row 6: knit.

Row 7: purl.

Row 8: k2, k2tog, k2.

Row 9: purl.

Row 10: k2, k2tog, k1.

Row 11: purl.

Row 12: k1, k2tog, k1.

Row 13: purl.

Row 14: sk2po.

Fasten off.

Make the stalk

Using green yarn and the 4mm (UK 8, US 6) DPN, cast on 2 sts.

Row 1: k2; do not turn but slide sts to other end of needle.

Repeat this until work measures approximately 5cm (2in).

Fasten off.

Using one of the tails, sew stalk to the top of the leaf.

Make the vine

Using green yarn and the
4mm (UK 8, US 6) DPN, cast
on 20 sts.

Cast off the 20 sts.

Fasten off.

Twist vine to help it 'curl'.

Attach the leaf and vine

Position the stalk and vine on
the base of the stem and sew
in place.

Work in ends neatly.

Harvest feast

*This simple, elegant cosy makes a
gorgeous table decoration ideal
for Thanksgiving celebrations or
Halloween parties.*

Christmas

Materials:

One ball each of red, green and white worsted-weight (UK Aran) yarn

Tapestry needle

Two stitch holders

Instructions:

Make two.

Using red yarn and 4mm (UK 8, US 6) needles, cast on 42 sts.

Work 14 rows in SS.

Change to white yarn and work 2 rows.

Change to green yarn and work 6 rows.

Change to white yarn and work 2 rows.

Change to red yarn and work 6 rows.

Change to white yarn and work 2 rows.

Change to green yarn and work 6 rows.

Change to white yarn and work 2 rows.

Change to red yarn and work 6 rows.

Change to white yarn and work 2 rows.

Change to green yarn and work 2 rows.

Shape the top

Row 1: continue with green yarn, k7, k2tog, *k6, k2tog*, rep from * to * to last st, k1.

Row 2: purl.

Row 3: k6, k2tog, *k5, k2tog*, rep from * to * to last st, k1.

Row 4: purl.

Row 5: change to white yarn and k5, k2tog, *k4, k2tog*, rep from * to * to last st, k1.

Row 6: purl.

Row 7: change to red yarn and k4, k2tog, *k3, k2tog*, rep from * to * to last st, k1.

Row 8: purl.

Row 9: k3, k2tog, *k2, k2tog*, rep from * to * to last st, k1.

Row 10: purl.

Row 11: k2, k2tog, *k1, k2tog*, rep from * to * to last st, k1.

Row 12: purl.

Needles:

One pair 4mm (UK 8, US 6) knitting needles

One pair 4mm (UK 8, US 6) DPN

Tension:

5 sts = 2.5cm (1in)

Row 13: change to white yarn and k1, k2tog, *k2tog*, rep from * to * to last st, k1.

Row 14: purl.

Row 15: knit.

Row 16: purl.

Row 17: knit.

Cut yarn and place sts on stitch holder.

Make up the cosy

Place the wrong sides of the cosy together (right sides facing out).

Sew the top

Thread a tapestry needle with one of the white tails at the top of the cosy.

Sew 7.5cm (3in) down one side.

Fasten off and hide tail in the seam.

Repeat on other side of cosy.

Sew the bottom

Thread the tapestry needle with one of the red tails of yarn from the cast on edge.

Sew up one side for 4cm (1½in).

Fasten off and hide tail in seam.

Repeat on the other side of cosy.

Make the curly top

Slip first st from stitch holder onto one of the 4mm (UK 8, US 6) DPN.

Row 1: with green yarn, work this stitch only and cast on 12 sts using the backward loop cast on.

Row 2: cast off the same 12 sts as tight as possible to make strands curl.

Row 3: knit next st from stitch holder to right needle.

Row 4: cast off first st over the second st (1 st remains on needle).

Repeat rows 1–4 across this and the remaining 5 sts on the stitch holder.

Cut yarn leaving 25cm (10in) tail.

Fasten off.

Repeat the above on the sts on the other st holder.

Sew the curly strands together

Using the picture as a guideline, thread green tail through tapestry needle and wind yarn tightly around the fourteen strands above the white section of the cosy to hold them securely together.

Hide tail down through the middle of the curly top and fasten under cosy.

Work in ends neatly.

Festive fun
This festive cosy features traditional colours as well as a bit of extra sparkle on top!

Cherry

Materials:

One ball each of green and white worsted-weight (UK Aran) yarn

Oddment of red worsted-weight (UK Aran) yarn

Two stitch holders

Polyester wadding

Needles:

One pair 4mm (UK 8, US 6) knitting needles

One pair 3.25mm (UK 10, US 3) DPN

Tension:

5 sts = 2.5cm (1in)

Instructions:

Make two.

Using green yarn and 4mm (UK 8, US 6) needles, cast on 42 sts.

Work 16 rows in SS.

Change to white yarn and work 8 rows.

Change to green yarn and work 8 rows.

Change to white yarn and work 8 rows.

Change to green yarn and work 8 rows.

Change to white yarn and work 2 rows.

Shape the top

Row 1: continue with white yarn, k7, k2tog, *k6, k2tog*, rep from * to * to last st, k1.

Row 2: purl.

Row 3: k6, k2tog, *k5, k2tog*, rep from * to * to last st, k1.

Row 4: purl.

Row 5: k5, k2tog, *k4, k2tog*, rep from * to * to last st, k1.

Row 6: purl.

Row 7: k4, k2tog, *k3, k2tog*, rep from * to * to last st, k1.

Row 8: purl.

Row 9: k3, k2tog, *k2, k2tog*, rep from * to * to last st, k1.

Row 10: purl.

Row 11: k2, k2tog, *k1, k2tog*, rep from * to * to last st, k1.

Row 12: purl.

Row 13: change to green yarn and k1, k2tog, *k2tog*, rep from * to * to last st, k1.

Row 14: purl.

Row 15: knit.

Row 16: purl.

Row 17: knit.

Cut yarn and place sts on stitch holder.

Make up the cosy

Place the wrong sides of the cosy together (right sides facing out).

Thread tapestry needle with the green tail on the back stitch holder.

Graft the sts on the stitch holders together.

Sew the top

Continue sewing with the tail down one side for 10cm (4in).

Fasten off, hide tail in seam.

Repeat on other side of cosy.

Sew the bottom

Thread the tapestry needle with one of the green tails of yarn from the cast on edge.

Sew up one side for 4cm (1½in).

Fasten off, hide tail in seam.

Repeat on other side of cosy.

Make the cherries

Make two.

Using red yarn and the 3.25mm (UK 10, US 3) DPN, cast on 10 sts.

Row 1: knit.

Row 2: purl.

Row 3: kfb in each st across row.

Row 4: purl.

Row 5: knit.

Row 6: purl.

Row 7: knit.

Row 8: purl.

Row 9: knit.

Row 10: purl.

Row 11: knit.

Row 12: purl.

Row 13: k2tog across row.

Thread tail through tapestry needle and draw through all sts pulling tight to secure.

Sew seam leaving a small opening at the top.

Lightly stuff cherries with wadding and finish sewing.

Work in ends neatly.

Make the strings

Using green yarn and the 3.25mm (UK 10, US 3) DPN, cast on 2 sts.

Row 1: k2; do not turn but slide sts to other end of needle.

Repeat this row until work measures approximately 10cm (4in).

Fasten off.

Using one of the tails, sew string to the top of the cherry.

With the other tail, sew string below the green section at the top of the cosy.

Work in ends neatly.

Make the leaves

Make two.

Using green yarn and the 3.25mm (UK 10, US 3) DPN, cast on 3 sts.

Row 1: knit.

Row 2: knit.

Row 3: k1, m1, k1, m1, k1.

Row 4: knit.

Row 5: k2, m1, k1, m1, k2.

Row 6: knit.

Row 7: k3, m1, k1, m1, k3.

Row 8: knit.

Row 9: k4, m1, k1, m1, k4.

Row 10: knit.

Row 11: knit.

Row 12: knit.

Row 13: k2tog, k7, k2tog.

Row 14: knit.

Row 15: k2tog, k5, k2tog.

Row 16: knit.

Row 17: k2tog, k3, k2tog.

Row 18: knit.

Row 19: k2tog, k1, k2tog.

Row 20: knit.

Row 21: sk2po.

Fasten off.

Attach the leaves

Position the leaves on the base of the green section and sew in place.

Work in ends neatly.

Very cherry

This homely cosy is simple, stylish and elegant and would make a great gift.

Apple

Materials:

One ball red worsted-weight (UK Aran) yarn

Oddments of worsted-weight (UK Aran) yarn in brown and green

Oddments of worsted-weight (UK Aran) yarn in white and black

Tapestry needle

Two stitch holders

Needles:

One pair 4mm (UK 8, US 6) knitting needles

One pair 4mm (UK 8, US 6) DPN

One pair 3.25mm (UK 10, US 3) DPN

Tension:

5 sts = 2.5cm (1in)

Instructions:

Make two.

Using red yarn and 4mm (UK 8, US 6) needles, cast on 42 sts.

Knit in SS until work measures 16.5cm (6½in) from the cast on edge.

Shape the top

Row 1: k7, k2tog, *k6, k2tog* rep from * to * to last st, k1.

Row 2: purl.

Row 3: k6, k2tog, *k5, k2tog*, rep from * to * to last st, k1.

Row 4: purl.

Row 5: k5, k2tog, *k4, k2tog*, rep from * to * to last st, k1.

Row 6: purl.

Row 7: k4, k2tog, *k3, k2tog*, rep from * to * to last st, k1.

Row 8: purl.

Row 9: k3, k2tog, *k2, k2tog*, rep from * to * to last st, k1.

Row 10: purl.

Row 11: k2, k2tog, *k1, k2tog*, rep from * to * to last st, k1.

Row 12: purl.

Row 13: k1, k2tog, *k2tog*, rep from * to * to last st, k1.

Row 14: purl.

Row 15: change to brown and k1, k2tog, k1, k2tog, k1.

Row 16: purl.

Row 17: knit.

Row 18: purl.

Row 19: knit.

Cut yarn and place sts on stitch holder.

Make up the cosy

Place the wrong sides of the cosy together (right sides facing out).

Thread tapestry needle with the brown tail on the back stitch holder.

Graft the sts on the stitch holders together.

Sew the stem

Continuing with the brown tail of yarn, sew down one side of the stem. Fasten off and hide tail in the seam.

Repeat on other side of stem.

Sew the top

Thread a tapestry needle with one of the red tails at the top of the cosy.

Sew down one side for 7.5cm (3in).

Fasten off, hide tail in seam.

Repeat on other side of cosy.

Sew the bottom

Thread the tapestry needle with one of the red tails of yarn from the cast on edge.

Sew up one side for 4cm (1½in).

Fasten off, hide tail in seam.

Repeat on other side of cosy.

Make the small leaf

Using green yarn and the 4mm (UK 8, US 6) DPN, cast on 4 sts.

Row 1: purl.

Row 2: k2, kfb, k1.

Row 3: purl.

Row 4: k2, kfb, k2.

Row 5: purl.

Row 6: knit.

Row 7: purl.

Row 8: k2, k2tog, k2.

Row 9: purl.

Row 10: k2, k2tog, k1.

Row 11: purl.

Row 12: k1, k2tog, k1.

Row 13: purl.

Row 14: sk2po.

Fasten off.

Make the large leaf

Using green yarn and the 4mm (UK 8, US 6) DPN, cast on 4 sts.

Row 1: purl.

Row 2: k2, kfb, k1.

Row 3: purl.

Row 4: k2, kfb, k2.

Row 5: purl.

Row 6: k2, kfb, k3.

Row 7: purl.

Row 8: knit.
Row 9: purl.
Row 10: k2, k2tog, k3.
Row 11: purl.
Row 12: k2, k2tog, k2.
Row 13: purl.
Row 14: k2, k2tog, k1.
Row 15: purl.
Row 16: k1, k2tog, k1.

Row 17: purl.
Row 18: sk2po.
Fasten off.

Attach the leaves

Position the leaves on the base of the stem and sew in place. Work in ends neatly.

Make the worm

Using white yarn and 3.25mm (UK 10, US 3) DPN, cast on 3 sts.

Row 1: k3; do not turn but slide sts to other end of the needle.

Repeat this row until work measures approximately 5cm (2in).

Using black yarn and tapestry needle sew small eye on one end.

Shape worm and sew on cosy.

An apple a day...

The wiggly worm adds a playful touch to this fruity cosy.

Carrots

Materials:

One ball of variegated green worsted-weight (UK Aran) yarn

Oddment of green worsted-weight (UK Aran) yarn

Oddment of orange double knitting (DK) yarn

Tapestry needle

Two stitch holders

Polyester wadding

Needles:

One pair 4mm (UK 8, US 6) knitting needles

One pair 4mm (UK 8, US 6) DPN

One pair 3.25mm (UK 10, US 3) kntting needles

Tension:

5 sts = 2.5cm (1in)

Instructions:

Make two.

Using green variegated yarn and 4mm (UK 8, US 6) needles, cast on 42 sts.

Knit in SS until work measures 15cm (6in) from the cast on edge.

Shape the top

Row 1: k7, k2tog, *k6, k2tog*, rep from * to * to last st, k1.

Row 2: purl.

Row 3: k6, k2tog, *k5, k2tog*, rep from * to * to last st, k1.

Row 4: purl.

Row 5: k5, k2tog, *k4, k2tog*, rep from * to * to last st, k1.

Row 6: purl.

Row 7: k4, k2tog, *k3, k2tog*, rep from * to * to last st, k1.

Row 8: purl.

Row 9: k3, k2tog, *k2, k2tog*, rep from * to * to last st, k1.

Row 10: purl.

Row 11: k2, k2tog, *k1, k2tog*, rep from * to * to last st, k1.

Row 12: purl.

Row 13: k1, k2tog, *k2tog*, rep from * to * to last st, k1.

Row 14: change to green and k1, k2tog, k1, k2tog, k1.

Row 15: purl.

Row 16: knit.

Row 17: purl.

Row 18: knit.

Row 19: purl.

Row 20: knit.

Do not cut yarn.

Place sts on stitch holder.

Make up the cosy

Place the wrong sides of the cosy together (right sides facing out).

Sew the top

Using one of the tails of the green variegated yarn, sew 7.5cm (3in) down one side of the cosy.

Fasten off, hide tail in seam.

Repeat on other side of cosy.

Sew the bottom

Thread the tapestry needle with one of the green variegated tails of yarn from the cast on edge.

Sew up one side for 4cm (1½in).

Fasten off, hide tail in seam.

Repeat on other side of cosy.

Make the stalks

Slip first st from stitch holder onto one of the 4mm (UK 8, US 6) DPN.

Row 1: continuing with the green yarn, work this stitch only and cast on 24 sts using the backward loop cast on.

Row 2: cast off the same 24 sts as tight as possible to make 'stalk' curl.

Row 3: knit next st from stitch holder.

Row 4: cast off first st over the second st (1 st remains on needle).

Repeat rows 1–4 across this and the remaining 3 sts on the stitch holder.

Cut yarn leave 25cm (10in) tail.

Fasten off.

Repeat the above on the sts on the other st holder.

Sew the stalks together

Using the picture as a guide, thread a green tail through tapestry needle and wind yarn tightly around the ten stalks of the cosy to hold them securely together. Hide tail down through middle of the stalks and fasten under cosy.

Work in ends neatly.

Make the carrots

For two carrots make four carrot shapes.

Using orange yarn and 3.25mm (UK 10, US 3) needles, cast on 2 sts.

Row 1: knit.

Row 2: purl.

Row 3: knit.

Row 4: purl.

Row 5: knit.

Row 6: purl.

Row 7: knit.

Row 8: purl.

Row 9: k1, m1, k1.

Row 10: purl.

Row 11: knit.

Row 12: purl.

Row 13: knit.

Row 14: purl.

Row 15: k1, m1, k1, m1, k1.

Row 16: purl.

Row 17: knit.

Row 18: purl.

Row 19: k1, m1, k3, m1, k1.

Row 20: purl.

Row 21: knit.

Row 22: purl.

Row 23: knit.

Row 24: purl.

Row 25: k1, k2tog, k1, k2tog, k1.

Row 26: Purl.

Row 27: k1, k2tog, k2.

Row 28: purl.

Row 29: k1, k2tog, k1.

Row 30: sk2po.

Fasten off.

Make three more halves.

With tails and tapestry needle, sew two halves together (right sides facing out) leaving a small opening at the top.

Lightly stuff carrots with wadding and finish sewing.

Work in ends neatly.

Make the strings

Using green yarn and 3.25mm (UK 10, US 3) needles, cast on 2 sts.

Row 1: k2; do not turn but slide sts to other end of needle.

Repeat this row until work measures approximately 17.5cm (7in).

Fasten off.

Using one of the tails, sew string to the top of the carrot.

With the other tail, sew string below the stem of the cosy.

Work in ends neatly.

Repeat for the second carrot.

Grow your own

This charming cosy is perfect for quirky, green-fingered gardeners.

Bee

Materials:

One ball each of black and yellow worsted-weight (UK Aran) yarn

Tapestry needle

Two stitch holders

Needles:

One pair 4mm (UK 8, US 6) knitting needles

One pair 4.5mm (UK 7, US 7) DPN

Tension:

5 sts = 2.5cm (1in)

Instructions:

Make two.

Using black yarn and 4mm (UK 8, US 6) needles, cast on 42 sts.

Work 16 rows in SS.

Change to yellow yarn and work 8 rows.

Change to black yarn and work 8 rows.

Change to yellow yarn and work 8 rows.

Change to black yarn and work 8 rows.

Change to yellow yarn and work 8 rows.

Shape the top

Row 1: change to black yarn and k7, k2tog, *k6, k2tog*, rep from * to * to last st, k1.

Row 2: purl.

Row 3: k6, k2tog, *k5, k2tog*, rep from * to * to last st, k1.

Row 4: purl.

Row 5: k5, k2tog, *k4, k2tog*, rep from * to * to last st, k1.

Row 6: purl.

Row 7: k4, k2tog, *k3, k2tog*, rep from * to * to last st, k1.

Row 8: purl.

Row 9: k3, k2tog, *k2, k2tog*, rep from * to * to last st, k1.

Row 10: purl.

Row 11: k2, k2tog, *k1, k2tog*, rep from * to * to last st, k1.

Row 12: purl.

Row 13: k1, k2tog, *k2tog*, rep from * to * to last st, k1.

Cut yarn and place sts on stitch holder.

Make up the cosy

Place the wrong sides of the cosy together (right sides facing out).

Thread tapestry needle with the black tail on the back stitch holder.

Graft the sts on the stitch holders together.

Sew the top

Continue sewing with the tail down one side for 7.5cm (3in).

Fasten off and hide tail in the seam.

Repeat on other side of cosy.

Sew the bottom

Thread the tapestry needle with one of the black tails of yarn from the cast on edge.

Sew up one side for 4cm (1½in).

Fasten off and hide tail in the seam.

Repeat on the other side of cosy.

Make the antennae

Make two.

Measure 2.5cm (1in) from centre top of cosy.

With black yarn and 4.5mm (UK 7, US 7) DPN pick up and knit 4 sts.

Row 1: k4; do not turn but slide sts to other end of needle.

Repeat this row until work measures 6cm (2½in).

Next row: kfb, k2, kfb, (6 sts); do not turn but slide sts to other end of needle.

Work two more rows even with these 6 sts.

Cut yarn leaving a 15cm (6in) tail.

With tapestry needle pull tail across the back and through the 6 sts.

Pull the tail down through the centre of the cord – pull it tight so that the antenna stands upright.

Secure tail underneath the cosy.

Repeat for other antenna.

Falling Leaves

Materials:

One ball burgundy worsted-weight (UK Aran) yarn

Oddments of green, ochre and brown worsted-weight (UK Aran) yarn

Tapestry needle

Two stitch holders

Needles:

One pair 4mm (UK 8, US 6) knitting needles

One pair 4mm (UK 8, US 6) DPN

Tension:

5 sts = 2.5cm (1in)

Instructions:

Make two.

Using burgundy yarn and 4mm (UK 8, US 6) needles, cast on 42 sts.

Knit in SS until work measures 16.5cm (6½in) from the cast on edge.

Shape the top

Row 1: k7, k2tog, *k6, k2tog*, rep from * to * to last st, k1.

Row 2: purl.

Row 3: k6, k2tog, *k5, k2tog*, rep from * to * to last st, k1.

Row 4: purl.

Row 5: k5, k2tog, *k4, k2tog*, rep from * to * to last st, k1.

Row 6: purl.

Row 7: k4, k2tog, *k3, k2tog*, rep from * to * to last st, k1.

Row 8: purl.

Row 9: k3, k2tog, *k2, k2tog*, rep from * to * to last st, k1.

Row 10: purl.

Row 11: k2, k2tog, *k1, k2tog*, rep from * to * to last st, k1.

Row 12: purl.

Row 13: k1, k2tog, *k2tog*, rep from * to * to last st, k1.

Cut yarn and place sts on stitch holder.

Make up the cosy

Place the wrong sides of the cosy together (right sides facing out).

Thread tapestry needle with the burgundy tail on the back stitch holder.

Graft the sts on the stitch holders together.

Sew the top

Continue sewing with the tail down one side for 7.5cm (3in).

Fasten off, hide tail in seam.

Repeat on other side of cosy.

Sew the bottom

Thread the tapestry needle with one of the burgundy tails of yarn from the cast on edge.

Sew up one side for 4cm (1½in).

Fasten off, hide tail in seam.

Repeat on other side of cosy.

Make the leaves

Make two.

Using green or ochre yarn and the 4mm (UK 8, US 6) DPN, cast on 3 sts.

Row 1: knit.

Row 2: knit.

Row 3: k1, m1, k1, m1, k1.

Row 4: knit.

Row 5: k2, m1, k1, m1, k2.

Row 6: knit.

Row 7: k3, m1, k1, m1, k3.

Row 8: knit.

Row 9: k4, m1, k1, m1, k4.

Row 10: knit.

Row 11: knit.

Row 12: knit.

Row 13: k2tog, k7, k2tog.

Row 14: knit.

Row 15: k2tog, k5, k2tog.

Row 16: knit.

Row 17: k2tog, k3, k2tog.

Row 18: knit.

Row 19: k2tog, k1, k2tog.

Row 20: knit.

Row 21: sk2po.

Fasten off.

Work in ends neatly.

Make the stalks

Make two.

Using green or ochre yarn and the 4mm (UK 8, US 6) DPN, cast on 2 sts.

Row 1: k2; do not turn but slide sts to other end of needle.

Repeat this row until work measures approximately 7.5cm (3in).

Fasten off.

Using one of the tails, sew stalk to the top of the leaf.

Make the vines

Make two.

With brown yarn and the 4mm (UK 8, US 6) DPN, cast on 20 sts.

Cast off the 20 sts.

Fasten off.

Twist vines to help them curl.

Attach the leaves and vines

Position the leaves and vines on the top of the cosy and sew in place.

Work in ends neatly.

Seasonal shades

The rich, warm shades make this cosy the ideal accompaniment to tea time when the evenings start to draw in.

Publishers' Note
If you would like more information on knitting techniques, try:
Knitting for the Absolute Beginner by Alison Dupernex,
Search Press, 2012;
Twenty to Make: Knitted Beanies by Susie Johns,
Search Press, 2012